The Shepherd Couple

and other poems

Poornima Dayal

BookLeaf
Publishing

India | USA | UK

Made with ❤ on the BookLeaf Publishing Platform
www.bookleafpub.in
www.bookleafpub.com

Dedication

I dedicate this book to the Almighty Lord for bringing experiences in my life that helped me write these poems.

Preface

This book is compilation of 21 poems. These poems are on varied themes, some highly imaginative and lucid in content.
Some of them reflect my feelings or thoughts while they were being written.

I have also tried to sum up some important life lessons in a poetic and rhythmic manner.
Poetry is very vast and seamless, exploring various emotions and situations in a poet's life, that may also reflect somewhere in the daily nuances of a reader's life.

The pronouns in some poems starting with capital letters refer to God.
There is also reference to the Divine, using archaic words in certain poems.

Thank you for picking up this book. Hope you enjoy reading it.

Acknowledgements

I am grateful to the Almighty Lord for helping me pen
these poems.
I also thank my son, my husband, my mother and my
loving pet for always being so supportive in my artistic
and poetic journey.

1. The Wind God

My dear Wind God
thanking You with a nod.
Washing away all thoughts and stories
wiping tears, reflecting Thy glory.

That waft of air, taking away cares
allowing myself to bask under the love You share.
Trees swish and swash
as memories are totally washed,
the Hibiscus, a dew drop White
or the Pansies oh, so light,
transforming the Earth and the mind,
You are just so very kind.
Joie de vivre, being grateful for what life offers,
it appears at this hour to be so proper..
Being thankful for every moment
for human endowments,
for giving us a heart and mind
for helping me move forward without a rewind.

Running my fingers smoothly through my curly strands,
wearing simple clothings of no heavy duty brands,
inhaling that smell, that tranquil air
walking as I do carefree but with a flair.

As You blow merrily
I live and breathe verily,
watching those petals gently swirl and move
caressing them slowly but swiftly as You choose.
The fragrance of Roses
dancing as they may be in poses
to the rhythm of Thy flow
as You, my Wind Gods blow.

Hearing your sounds
keeps me on the ground,
mountains letting go their frowns
as in Your subtility, perhaps, their woes they drown.

I see that manger,
with an almost broken hanger,
as I am ready to feed the animal,
isn't nature just so phenomenal.
As You blow from right to left,
- from left to right
or wherever takes You, Your invisible might

the animals breathe,
they have no creed
plentiful air
with no despair,
ha, no, am not talking out of thin air.

That day I remember
or was it a morning in November,
when walking to the gate
I did think of a debate
not pleasant, nor happy was it a thought
but in Your flow and blow, refuge I sought.
Cleansing and nourishing me that day
thankful am I forever, for leading my way.

Wind Gods You blow and rise above,
teaching me silence and the ways to self Love.

2. Memories of Kashmir

Amidst the bountiful valleys of Kashmir,
was this capped man resembling a fakir,
selling Willow wood cricket bats
on a stand that usually sold hats.
Close to him, climbing a Deodar tree were tiny tots
wearing loose shirts and dirty, small, Woolen shorts.

My brother, about 16, buying one of those bats,
with my dad, began to chat.
As I Picked up some colourful pebbles
before the river waters bubbled,
and some near by forgs gurgled.
A passion with me when I was about five,
such trips kept me going, they kept me alive.
As we cheered,
looking around without any fear,
appreciating the fauna and flaura,
this city and its magnificent aura,
climbing some slopes
or traveling by the rope,

admiring the Roses, Tulips or Blue Poppies,
clicking many pictures and even making copies.

My Shikara, a rustic Red and painted Green
a youngish, smart boatman, tall and lean.
His long, loose Pheran, a Beigish Brown
and as he yawned, I noticed a slight frown.
Toiling night and day,
in Monsoon, Summer till May
resting at times on a nearby mount of hay.
Crossing the Jhelum, of melted snow it is,
a fascinating experience, with no fuzz or fizz.
Nature's magnanimity,
blessing all humanity
watching more decorated boats,
as my shikara gently floats.

Running enthusiastically
from behind a narrow gully,
came this thin, short bearded man
of visiting tourists was he a fan.
A villager perhaps, from a humble dwelling
inviting us to his home, and he started belling.
A wife so serene,
had I hardly seen
sitting, puffing at the fire place,
whilst their children were outside running a short race.

Her light Pink, embroidered Kaftan, covered by a thin, Pink shawl,
with mirrors and laces around its fall.
Offering us some warm Kahwa and tasty delicacies to eat,
we were thanking the the Lord for such mercies and unimaginable meets.
Served in a steel bowl was the Gushtaba with succulent pieces,
which she laid on crochet mats, without any creases.
The Tabak Maz was seasoned with pepper,
there couldn't have been anything then much better.
Kashmiri hospitality and warmth is gracious
forever in my mind are etched those memories, so precious.
A simple man with no ulterior motives,
inviting us to enjoy and share was his only motive.
No money, no greed, asking no favours,
as we relished and cherished such delectable flavours.

Leaving soon for Pehelgam from Shrinagar by car,
not a very long trip, yes, it wasn't so far.

Reminiscing those carefree days
when man had easier ways
to play and feel joy,
when love and care weren't treated as mere toys.

Hoarding those pebbles that stood the test of time,
as some people kept diluting their drinks with more Gin
and Thyme.

3. Bringing light to a child's life

Bring light to a child's life,
do a dance, a little jive
speaking with him in childlike ways,
listening to his tales
while sitting under the tree he regales.

Be a child, be very mild
play with him, somewhere in the wild.

I see his crisp, cotton shirt,
while he enjoys, feeling no hunger nor thirst.
Pulling a toy, tied fast on a rope
bringing him joy and lots of hope.
A cart made with pieces of wood,
painted Red, Yellow and Green
with wheels being pulled, it has a certain sheen.
In the evening, he walks, when its nearing dusk
while munching on fragments of Coconut, without its
husk.

Lost in a world of his own
his knickers are Black and slightly torn,
with patches of White
resembling the shape of a kite,
and time is quickly moving from evening to night.

Washing my hands, wriggling my fists
joining him to hear his tales and twists,
surrounding him are more boys from his village
eating some groundnuts are they, avoiding spillage.

A lad of ten,
walking towards his den
in those forest like Green woods
where once a tree perhaps stood.
Speaking of his 'Amma', he whistles and gestures,
talking is he of fond memories of old pastures,
of his cows and calves
and some baked bread loafs cut into halves.
He mentions her bright, Pink Sari
with prints of the Moon and a night very starry,
her lips painted Red by chewing Beetal,
stitching clothes with her thin thread and needle.
Clapping my hands aloud I cheer,
hearing his tales as I am too near.
A tiny little Brown bird pecks and begs,
as it comes and sits close to his legs.

His pet may be,
its just a little baby.

His toy now lies on the side,
in a small little hole, a place where it hides.
Mahesh, Krish and Ramesh are his friends
hearing him too are they or so they pretend,
sitting with folded legs, palms cupping their chins
as he speaks now of his granny with a grin.

I offer him my box of toffees
devoid are they of any coffee,
tasting more like Lemonade,
which he relishes sitting under a gigantic tree shade.

'Thumba'- 'Thumba', as his Mumma calls
he gets up, almost avoiding a fall,
gripping a branch, beginning to again pull his toy
he is surely an obedient but playful young, boy.

Bringing light to a child's life,
is surely reviving our own lives.

4. India, I love you

My India, I love you so much,
like a mother, you are, with a holy touch.

Your fancy colours and radiant skyline,
full of mirth is your land, its supremely divine.
Calling me into your lap
as I run and hug you, no its not any trap.
Pinks, Mauves and Yellow Sunflowers,
and farmers working around the clock, at every hour.
Tilling the land, sowing rich seeds
exporting almost all crops, does India lead.
Growing on tall or medium stalks
are good Wheat stems,
resembling are they Citrine and other gems.

Our bowl of bounties is perennialy full
oh, India towards you I will always have this pull.
Come January to May
are rich harvests full of gay,
and September to December

are festivals that we always remember.

Fragrant spices, like cardamom or Corriander,
perhaps in national parks are also roaming some large
Elephants and Reindeer.
Love for Tigers and Lions like such
is rarely seen
in restoring wild life, are Indians keen.

A dash of pungent, Red chillies
no artificial stuff or those frillies,
baked Gram flour and crushed Black, Peppercorns
added to breads and some rustling popcorns.
Abundant varieties
and worshiping the dieties,
temples so decorated,
and they are rightly highly rated.
The sounds of ringing bells,
pounding Wheat smells,
Granny's hoarse voices,
just so many choices.
The feeling of belonging
for which we are always longing,
those settled in foreign lands may feel
India is what they need to love and to heal.

Its Holi, Diwali, Christmas or Eid

dressed and ready are people before they proceed
to temples, mosques or churches alike
such amazing faith and glory that we always like.

There may be somewhere this so called poverty,
but theres love, liberty, fraternity and harmony.
Of Snake charmers was known this Indian land
today victorious in most avenues do we stand.
Traditions so vast
from every corner do they last
multicolored are fabrics,
to culture and arts do we stick.
Hardworking like Beavers
are our very Indian weavers,
interlacing two sets of threads
preparing clothings for the newly weds.
Gigantic are their looms,
on which a fabric grooms
moving back and forth, in slow motion,
threads passing in slow rotations.

Rich is our heritage,
its timeless gems known since ages,
the Kohinoor did once belong
to our country for so long.

The tastes of Samosas, mixed Pakodas, hot Rasam and

Idli's,
to Kahwa's, Dhoklas and breads toasted so mildly,
served with pickles of stewed Lemon and Mango
doesn't always have to be these two to tango.

Grandpa's fond remembrance
without any encumberance,
Grannys old tales
before which all fails.
Mothers and fathers holding their children
in teens or more and even when they have
grandchildren.
Such love and bonds are never seen
in any other land even with any shimmer or sheen.

With fields in plenty,
folks carelessly strolling even in their twenties,
where women chew beetal,
and flutes loudly tweetle.
The splutering and fluttering of Mustard seeds,
being roasted or cooked, before a young mom feeds.

Oh India, my country in you I take pride,
you dress me daily, like your own precious bride.
In garments of Cotton, Raw Silk or Tussar
this is just a short poem, unfolding a movie like a
precursor.

5. Beauty Pageants

Dressing up may be your passion,
wearing and draping the best in fashion
look at the mirror and you will find
that pretty face, oh so kind.
Love it more and let it know
allow the seeds for self love to sow.
You are a queen, and you must believe
no judges, nor opinions do you need.
Walk lovingly the ramp of your heart,
blowing flying kisses to every part,
showing off that smile, thats so real
and now you must make that a deal.
Clapping hands and cheering yourself loud,
do not wait for comments from any crowds
of your gorgeousness, you should be proud.

Foundations, mascaras, concelaers do you require?,
thank the Divine whose light we accquire.
Dont wait for any approvals, my awesome girl,
the world may else ask you to twirl or whirl.

Trust your creator to know your truth,
loving yourself every moment, in old age or in youth.

A beauty pageant within your home
walking up to the mirror as you comb.
Must you ask how you look
or consider matching some fancy book
with models dolling up to suit
every role offered to them as they shoot.
Be your queen and own yourself,
let no suggestions matter, embrace the self.
Ofcourse, put on your best, if you must
allowing the mind to fully love and trust.
You are a winner
you need not be more thinner
than the body can cope
thats just not done, nope!
Loving the body,
without considering it gaudy,
treating it with care
and more love with yourself you
share.
Go buy your trophy if you please,
more clothes or gifts to self appease.
If that brings joy, then so mote be
no more contests or competitions, setting yourself free.

6. Women's Day

They call it Women's day today
every day is a celebration, from Monday to Sunday.
The reward of this awesome heart,
from motherly feelings, do we never part.
To continue living life,
without showing off any strive,
a quiet winner,
with that mascara and eye liner.
The subtilities of every heartbeat and breath,
caring and doing forever, without any fears of death.
A wish for myself and others today
is to take care and love ourselves more today and
everyday,
to love and elope with the self,
picking up the best path for ourselves,
leading us to immense contentment and inner joy,
a feeling so pure, of no longer playing coy.

Hugging ourselves this very day
come yesterday, today or just any day.

Learning from our dear mothers
the knack of self respect and such from others.
Standing up always for ourselves,
not putting our beliefs beneath all or any shelves
rejoicing our bodies and it's bio rhythms
their isn't any mathematics to this or algorithms.

Woman, you are forever blessed,
let none make you ever feel any less.
Shine, rise without any fright
you are strong, just feel your gorgeous might.

Thankful to my Earthly mother,
for bringing me up and my elder brother
teaching us to study and play
taking care of us every night and day.
My lacy frocks,
with my curly locks,
dressing me up
like her tiny, girl cub.
Learning, unlearning what what life did sew
many a lessons, ha, there weren't just a few
but it was fun,
while I ate those hearty Jam buns
feasting on those lessons ,
many naturally grooming sessions
within the magnificent confines of my salon called life,

with pedicures, manicures and waxing using blunt
knives,
learning to care and caress
as I washed and conmbed my every tress.

I am this woman, a child of my holy mother,
my Goddess, Divine
so very sublime,
You always shine,
taking me in Thy Godly arms
besotted am I by Your delightful charm.
I am the feminine,
with nothing thats truly mine
its all Her delightful glory,
living within whom are we this life's story.

7. The Shepherd couple

Crossing was I this lightly, Green belt
returning from Lonavala, when I smelt
this sweet and milky aroma
of Corn being roasted by this little girl Shoma.
Many more vendors selling their goods
as I crossed in my Red car, wearing a Linen jacket with a
soft hood.

Admiring the countryside, driving ahead across the
ghats
watching Ripe Guavas being sold on some Wooden carts.
A couple so traditional did I see
walking behind their Sheep with so much glee.
Crumpled, light Brown shirt
with a plain, White dhoti tied around his girth,
a Nehru cap adorning his crown
climbing a hillock is he, away from the town.
His Black and White Sheep,
are grazing, ascending the hills quite steep.
'Sujata', as he lovingly calls his wife

joining him, she's very much a part of his life.
Her light Turq Sari, flying delicately in the air,
humming a tune is she without any care.
Some ripe Mangoes in her bag she's carrying
also preparing for her daughter who will soon be
marrying.

Living in conditions not known to me,
lessons to learn from them do we have for free.
His staff is tall and Maroon in colour
holding as though he's won a trophy for valour.
Moving behind them towards lush pastures,
following the Sheep, like they are his Masters.

Such appealing sights did I see
while having a sandwich in my car with some hot tea.
Slowly moving, holding my phone
aiming and clicking, may not be as clear as with a Drone.

8. Last of the royals

The bejewelled crown
now a part of the historic London town,
carved in Gold and precious stones
the rich, royal English county now does own.

A glowing red skull cap, its not ordinary
worn once by an Indian king, not just by all and sundry.
With shimmering Turquoise, Rubies and Pearls,
Diamonds, Emeralds on high class Velvet, do unfurl
a royal legacy of bygone times
when kings and other nobility were in their primes.

The last of the mughal emperors,
known for poetry, as a great calligrapher.
A devout Sufi, almost a pir
before ascension, living like a fakir.
Once a whirling dervish, immersed in prayers
finding such a king then, was so rare.
Appearing of spare figure and stature,
humbly dressed, orthodox was he by nature.

No barriers, he said - Hinduism and Islam be alike
following multi cultures and such did he like.
Lyrical nizams and ghazals did he write,
perhaps, tough within this poem to summarize.

The glowing crown,
now a part of the historic London town,
a fragrant legacy,
an alluring treasury,
siezed and taken over in the rebellion,
sold was it to an English major like a medallion.

9. Boy in Blue

Ah, that delicious, Ice lolly
he was having, feeling completely jolly.
As I Crossed his home, a tiny shanty
while he smiled and beamed, enjoying that Ice candy.
Wearing a Royal Blue T shirt
above his small, Black knickers,
that Ice cream dripping
as he continued licking.
His brother was calling or perhaps it was his friend,
under the Sky Blue canopy, was he trying to bend.
Enjoying those flavours,
disinterested was he in granting any favours.

Admiring and smiling, as I wave out to him
sucking and slurping is he, filling up his tummy perhaps
to its brim.
Such carefree joys,
where children get to rejoice,
partaking such sweet treats,
skipping and jumping as their innocent heart beats.

A boy of about eight,
not worried about his weight,
chewing off the ice
bite by bite, as though it's a precious prize.
Holding it high, as it melts and drips
into his mouth, hes wiping off his lips.

Taking out my phone, I click this boy in Blue,
the Sun reflecting and casting, it's stunningly vibrant
rainbow hues.

10. Holy month of Ramadan

Sehri - Sehri, alarms ring,
sisters, wives and mothers bring
Silver plates with hot and fresh milk to drink.
Morning, evening churning a feast,
as women toil hard in their kitchens, for some it may be
a feat.
Yet hearts so pure, overflowing with passion
the holy month of Ramadan, is followed with extreme
devotion.
Sweeping, cleaning, wiping the kitchens clean
laying the mats and large plates, before the family eats.
Children may be scrambling out of their beds,
while men get dressed to pray on mats
woven with colorful threads.
Those embroidered abayas, covering their heads
heating left over Red meats, women are buttering the
breads.

Sweet smells of Sewaiyan and rich, roasted paranthas,
drowsy tiny tots, clinging on to their akas.

Tea cups clinking,
with few stars still twinkling,
pots and pans with them
are women bringing
as the night recedes,
into a long day does it proceed.

Calling out for prayers at the break of dawn,
before the gardener may be coming for mowing the
lawn.
Recited at the mosque, so fervently
a gathering of people praying reverently.

Passing the day in rest and worship
asking for pardon,
a life devoid of any hardship.
Going by daily routines,
children get ready for school, some may be in teens.
No hunger, no thirst does ever matter
a desirable time away from any usual chatter.

Evening is approaching, the day draws to a close
running home are they, thanking the Lord, for them He
chose.
Following their faith in the only one,
offering thanks for all that is being done.

Fried, grilled or baked treats
having now prayed are people running to eat.
A blessed month when the Quran did first descend,
honestly worshiping are followers,
hoping for a holy ascend.
Asking for Allah's everflowing mercies to never cease,
to help them live a life of love, as the Lord may please.

11. Sitting in the verandah

Sitting in the verandah,
sipping a hot cup of tea,
somewhere linning in the oblivion
is the shimmery Blue and Green Sea.

I see beyond the buildings
a faint demarcation,
between the Sea and land,
not really near my location,
joyful rays of the sun, casting their radiation
above the Ocean waters,
almost leading to some revelation.
Pearls upon pearls
glittering across the waves,
as new travels and voyages unfurl.
Summer is approaching,
a lovely, warm afternoon
inspiring me to wish you a loving Goodafternoon,
Its a Sunday and I am home
sitting in the verandah,

watching waves rinse the shore like translucent, White
foam.

A knitted tray lieing next to me
storing pots and plants, hovering above which are
twinkling, Red Honey bees.
Swarming, dancing perhaps collecting
this Sunny, bright day are they nonchalantly enjoying.
A light Pink Bougainvillea
hosting some Yellow butterflies,
its a treat to watch such alluring mother Nature, as time
gently flies.

Writing poetry gives me relief
from the day that may have been, from those moments,
even though they were brief.
The small but friendly Chikoo tree
flourishing, with its tiny fruits,
small Brown peels
from within which the fleshy fruit reveals.
Its not too sweet
but I merrily repeat
peeling, yet another
for my Divine, holy mother.

Tall palms swinging along Black railings,
of high rise, Grey and White buildings

and though they were resting,
but now they seem awake
perhaps, its the winds,
and for them theres nothing really at stake.

I hear the sounds of horns,
some cars at a distance
belching loud noises, as though its a scorn.
Sitting by myself in the verandah
can be so much fun
appreciating such sounds and even noises, no its not a
pun.

12. The Gift

Not obsessed with the body, but grateful for it
every part and organ is divinely lit
as I bow to the magnitude of such grace
with love and joy is it laced.
Surrendering to His will keeps it healthy,
allowing us to enjoy experiences that are wealthy .

Each bone and muscle sings Thy glory
hearing am I holy tales and stories.
The hands are precious, they help us perform
helping us touch and feel every form.
The feet let us proceed on life's paths,
a precious gift given, that we hath.
The cells may be shinning
like a silver linning,
those tissues and joints
reminding us at every point,
within Him is our existence
without any insistence,
the only truth

no need to play a sleuth.

My eyes help me see Thy brilliant spark,
the ears, helping us even hear sweet songs of the small
Lark.
With so much ease did he create,
and again and again does He recreate.
Without any tinge
are lit even the hinge,
oiled and resurrected,
so supremely constructed.

Such marvel, such amazement
at Thy wonders and placements,
oh Lord such a structure
with You as its conductor.

Not obsessed with the body, but grateful for it,
for every organ, sense organ, for every bit.

13. Love has finally found me

Its not so absurd
for me to write one or two words,
in humility or in gratitude,
theres just so much latitude.
Enhancing and lacing some facts
with real or imaginary acts.
Writing about the Lord,
I always hear a nod,
coming from within
expressing what lies therein.

My hearts a swimming pool
though never do I drown,
its private, just for me
wearing a hat do I, as my crown.
Filled with love for my children
and a few brethren,
it's waters are clear Blue
theres love for me and you.

Effervescent in nature,
to my feelings does it cater.
No sharks, no String rays
no strangers, no so called fakes.
Cleaned everyday and night
by the Sun and Moon rays, so bright.
Songs of devotion and love, thus it sings
affection and warmth with it, the heart brings.
Embracing me in it's cosy light
as though it was my romantic, loving knight
at times when I may seek, during the day or at night.
There may have been tough times,
lets not even try to find its rhyme,
no point in remembering,
whats over is over,
its time for a make over.

Some friends were mermaids,
or heroines of fairy tales,
some may have been cowboys or some friendly, casual
males.
Now my heart has grown up to love, disown and detach
learning that theres really nothing to ever get attached.
Love has finally, perhaps found me
theres His love and light that surrounds me.
My heart beats to his name

chanting it fervently is almost my only aim.

14. Out of shackles

Out of shackles,
flowing out of all that crackles.
Out of boundaries,
towards the seamless,
like waters after the shores,
beyond histories or folklore.
The rising Sun, upon the oceans
calming down minds, all those erosions
as I walk past that old, known joy
without completely letting those memories destroy.

Passions are wild,
the hearts so mild
walking on the bare sands,
merrily holding hands
into comforting pastures,
filled with loving gestures.
Beginnings may be many,
bringing me back every penny.
As love beckons

in new shapes and forms,
silencing all past storms.

Out of shackles...out of boundaries

Its over - and I have finally found these.

15. The womanly way

Reaching a stage of disdain?,
I know am not trying to abstain.
Its just a womanly thing, perhaps
to grow out of those lustful traps.
Times gone by, of feeling the pull
of living those moments, almost to the full.

Its not disdain, just a change in hormones,
from that desiring and aspiring, have I grown.
It was fun while it lasted,
not that its completely over or entirely blasted.
May be the way I am feeling today,
moods can be many, its the human way.

Appreciating these changes,
there may be so many ranges,
a woman learns to gently accept,
its not a challenge nor a secret well kept.

Moving on with grit and might,

embracing the Sun, nice and bright
thanking Divine for His Holy light
breathing and revering am I, every day and night.

16. Naayni

Picking up the frills of her skirt,
wiping of the soils and some dirt,
the Cotton, Pink napkin flying in the air,
hidden beneath is her scanty, Black hair.
Putting some flowers and fruits in that basket,
carrying a flask and a tiny, lacy casket..

'Naayni', 'Naayni'.....Lunia calls out,
approaching her grandma,
in excitement she shouts.
The smell of sweet cakes
which her loving mom baked,
as she brings to her granny,
holding hands of her sweet mother Fanny.

Amidst those musty hills,
in between which are many huge wind mills,
this thin, old lady toils day and night
pruning the grasses, she's of medium height.
That charming smile

can be noticed from a mile,
her teeth, like melting snow flakes
some chipped, few broken and some are fakes.

And when the work is over, atop the slopes she lies
closing her eyes meekly, under those clean, Grey- Blue
skies.
Years, its been,
the chores don't end, it seems
relentless is she, yet she often beams,
across such valleys since by gone years
where she once danced and laughed with her peers..

Afar at a distance,
singing and dancing are children to folk songs,
its been minutes and hours, oh, its been so long.

Traversing these lands
where the mountains still stand,
hoping He's ready to lift her with His gentle, soft hands.

17. Merged

Egos burning to ashes
in pure Fires, at the blink of eye lashes
as death doth them apart
the body and the soul do part.

A revered creation,
the body, enjoying recreation.
The soul remaining untarnished,
the living body does it varnish.

As flames rise high,
bidding some heartfelt goodbyes,
dancing and glowing
is the soul beaming
recognizing its merger, is it gleaming.
Of the Divinity
within its sublimity
does it rest,
leaving any boundaries of seeming arrest.
This loud merry making may be heard

as mankind makes way from its herd,
clapping victoriously, its hands so fair,
oh it was a ride in some theatrical affair.
Yet, thanking the Lord for his mercies
the glowing light, even more,
now it perceives.
Such applause, such gratitude never before was seen
for its time on Earth, for what may have been.

18. Ready to paint.

Is it romance that I may be seeking,
whatever it may be, its slightly sneaking.
C'mon its not a void,
perhaps, something or someone am I just trying to
avoid?.
Romance is in the Divine,
searching no longer for it, am I, even in any ravine.
Thanking God for this gift
for nothing more can uplift
the heart or the mind,
do I comfort myself, as I remind.

What's its about, a lonely feeling, perhaps not,
no, its not revealing.
Validation was enough,
no its not about that or anything tough.
Highlighting in indirect ways,
is it about some friends or lovers from past days?.
Closing many chapters,
it may be about characters

having no place
yet forming a case?.
Doubting such reasons for aches or hurts
it's better to move on without analyzing, yes, its not
worth.

Wondering what will flow next
on canvas or may be on paper as written text.
Changing the desk for keeping my paints
may just be an excuse, and now there is just no restraint.

As I Pick up - pick up - pick up the paint.

19. Moving on

Is life approaching an end,
there may have been few twists and bends.
Surrounding ourselves with people we love
and things we do that keep us in love.
Age may not be a barrier,
to enjoy and live a life much happier.
The end doesn't have to reflect
there may still be lots of time left.

Stop pondering over death or arranging for it,
relishing every moment while living every bit.
Sitting by my window, watching Black crows and cows
for every situation, seeds we seemingly sow.

Death may be faint, at a distance perhaps,
lingering in the oblivion, about it don't harp.
Watching transient movements of passers by, am I
there would still be promising moments, don't cry.

Another twenty or thirty years may be,

laughing is important, just be carefree,
breathing in those fragrant wisps of air,
baking, are some vendors Vanilla cakes in layers.
Munching roasted, Yellow Grams, as I do,
along with a hot cup of freshly made brew.
Nothing happens without a reason,
it's just a bit before the flowering season.

I am a poet, or may be not
writing verses and stories, lest I forgot
episodes or lessonss from my life,
narrating stazas, in the mornings quite bright.
An artist at times,
also scribbling these rhymes,
drawing and painting, it's not always a fine line.

Days are gently moving into the nights,
interlacing between the dark and the light.
There's still time, my friend
its not yet the end
do not hasten so much to make amends.
Wait a bit more, don't run away
its your time to shine, come March, April or May.

You may just be in your middle age
and even if its your ripe old age,
sing and dance like never before

to enchanting songs or some folklore.
If you feel it comes knocking your door,
be grateful for every second, life was good for sure.
Filled with light and blessings always
moving on is the Divine's surest ways,
ensuring that we forever rest
within him,
this life, no, its not a test.

20. A peeping Plant

My peeping plant,
I love you so
since the time, the seeds, did the gardener sow
Today, you are tall, its been five years
tons of love to you and a loud cheer.
Having grown in a muddy, soft bed
as it's glistening rays, does the Sun shed
when its morning,
new leaves may be adorning
your stems so long and slim,
I refuse to let him trim.
Those delicate petals, growing straight
or flowers so fragrant, there must right now be about
eight.

Peeping, laughing through the window,
dancing, rejoicing as those swift winds blow.
You hear my woes and see me smile,
my loving, dear friend, I see you from even more than a
mile.

Tell me stories that you may have heard,
planted outside are you,
listening to whispers and many words
of floating clouds, bringing forth rain
or birds in plenty, perched closed to the window pane.
Tell me how you date
the plant next to you, do you mate?.
We must talk and communicate
its such a pleasant, human trait.

Petting you every early morning
trees may be swaying, when Cuckoos must be humming.
You may have had dreams or fantasies you may have
lived,
my nature friend, I thank you, for the joys that you do
give.
Embracing your womb,
within mother Earth did you groom.
Watering you often
the soil, does it soften.
As saplings grow, beaming at the skies
reminding us of our holy ties,
those leaves so Green
under the Moonlight do they gleam,
basking in its illuminating glory,
almost about to reveal some enchanting story.

Come rain and I hold you close
let thunder not spoil that charming pose.
Feed me love, oh my lasse
before this moment or this time so easily passes.
You have a place in my heart
oh, my peeping plant I won't ever let you apart.

My peeping plant, I brush you everyday,
my caring fingers, on those leaves, as they play.

21. Love beckons

Love beckons us to follow His grace
may the Lord, God be praised.
Holding our hands, leading us on
across lofty lands , upon sands or dust
leaning upon him, we must.

As He speaks to us, through his voice of love
we kneel and pray, with eyes gazing above,
clearing our path, as He does
helping us sail , as in Him we trust.

A Silken, woven cloth draped on my altar,
blessing us is He, lest we falter.
In His Holy palms are invisible pearls
of mercy, love - and oh, my heart swirls.
Gathering us within His embrace,
washing - harmonizing, giving us our place.
Wiping tears, of sadness or despair
for laughter in our hearts, does he prepare.

Like a shinning Oyster, above the Blue Ocean
His waters bathing us in true devotion.
Melting desires,
dropping them in the hot, burning fires.
With wishes flying high on His sublime wings,
bringing our way is He love and lovable things.

As I step upon this land and Earth
bearing fruits, is he bestowing us mirth,
walking upon his land so tender
this gift of life to us, does he render.

A praise on my lips, every noon and day
worshiping Him, I am, under the Sun's magnificent rays.